Alan F Rees was born and raised in Townhill, Swansea and went on to serve as a regular soldier in the Royal Engineer Regiment from 1955-1958. He then went on to own his own business and invented a unique radiator valve which went on to be stocked in several DIY stores across the UK.

Alan started writing song lyrics in the early 1970's submitting them to publishers, but it was after his wife Linda started her second degree in English Literature that his poetry journey began.

After attending one of Swansea poetry collective, Poets on the Hill's workshops, meeting fellow poets, and partaking in performances he also met Pulpworm Publishing and now his debut collection is here.

Happy 60th BIRTHDAY
TO JANE.

Alan F Rees

This edition published by Pulpworm Limited

pulpwormlimited@gmail.com

Pulpworm Limited
32 Gwysfa Road, Ynystawe, Swansea, SA6 5AE

Cover Design by Stuart Lloyd Associates Ltd

ISBN PAPERBACK: 978-0-9955972-1-1

WHY?
By Alan F. Rees

Poems

O.T.T   **6**

The Poppies   **10**

The Untold Tales   **11**

Flanders Field   **15**

Frustration   **17**

14-18   **20**

The Sniper   **21**

Trench Foot   **23**

What They Really Were   **25**

Lions Led by Donkeys   **29**

The Marksman   **38**

They Made Us What We Are   **41**

The Contradictions   **44**

One Soldier's Story   **47**

Start as You Intend to Go On   **51**

They Did Their Bit   **53**

The Unknown Soldier   **57**

The End   **60**

The End Game- 1915   **62**

They Will Never Be the Same   **65**

The Silent Sentry   **68**

The Charge   **71**

It Cannot Go On   **74**

Christmas 1914- The Medic   **77**

You Cannot Take Anything for Granted   **81**

They Led and they Bled   **84**

Numbers   **88**

Will We Never Learn   **91**

Make of It What You Wish   **93**

The Extra Enemies   **96**

Uncovered   **99**

Why?   **100**

O.T.T

It was the worst kept secret
Because everybody knew
A half an hour before sunrise
Our next attack was due.

The signal to get started
Was when the whistle blew
But the whistles were so loud
The other side could hear them too.

And where we had to climb out
Run over open ground
The Germans stayed in cover
And tried to shoot us down.

And so, we stood and waited

Like so many hapless sheep
Each man afraid that he might have
A date with death to keep.

Some just smoked and waited
Others bowed their heads to pray
All of us were terrified
But no-one dared to say.

Then the wait was over
The whistles started to blow
And we scrambled up the trench sides
It was time for us to go.

My best friend was right in front of me
And as he reached the crest
I heard the thwack of a bullet
As it hit him in the chest.

He fell straight back on top of me

And bore me to the ground

Into six inches of wet mud

Where wounded men had drowned.

I panicked as I struggled, fighting to get free

My friend and his equipment, were all tangled up
in me.

And then I realised that my closest friend was
dying

And before I knew it, I was crying, crying, crying.

Then all at once and all around

The trenches are refilled

As our boys tumbled back in

Those who had not been killed.

Someone pulled Jim's body off

I staggered to my feet

My friend had saved me from the charge

And also, the retreat.

Officers were shouting

Men were coming from the back

To help us to repulse

The next counter attacks.

I looked up at the sky

It was lightening, pink and grey

And I prepared myself to face

Another bloody day.

The Poppies

They grew in haphazard profusion, simply
scattered around,

in singles and groups--all sown in confusion and
spread over the ruined ground.

Their centres shining black their petals a unique
shade of red,

if counted, maybe one poppy grew--for each young
soldier dead.

The Untold Tales

When words of war are written- they tell of the
soldiers, their struggles and pain

Of the wounded and of course those, who will
never come home again.

They write about the pathos, about the horror and
the fear

They write of what they hope and believe- will
advance their fame and career.

But they rarely write the stories that are not so
simple to find

No one writes of the problems faced by those who
are left behind.

For these are mundane stories that many of their
readers will share

No one writes or talks of them, but that doesn't
mean the stories aren't there.

No one writes of the mothers of children, who
could be left to bring them up alone

Of the constant, destructive fear- that he may never be coming back home.

She never now looks into the mirror for fear of what she might see

And she cannot stop her mind from wondering- whatever is going to be?

How she lays in that lonely bed at night- too tired to go to sleep

With it all to do tomorrow again- she can't let the little ones see her weep.

What of the nearly eighteen-year-old- counting as the days go by

In a mix of fear and excitement- not believing that he really could die.

He hopes he will do his duty, not be a coward and try to run

As children, they loved to play soldiers, but then it was a wooden gun.

He wonders how he will cope if he lives- but though alive- still comes to harm

Last week he saw one of the older boys, who'd been burned and lost an arm.

There is the young man who appears so healthy

But when tested- the doctors hear his heart murmur 'No way.'

But the looks of strangers, they pass him in the street

Ask 'Why is he still at home and not with the others away?'

Do they even think about the young woman- her life turned upside-down?

And the young man she thought may be the one- but who now is no longer around.

But she is determined to do her bit, in any way she can

Willingly now in a factory, doing work she hates- that should have been done by a man.

They don't write about the eight or nine-year-old, what is going on in his mind?

If you could enter his head- who can know exactly what you'd find.

Almost certainly thoughts of his Dad as a hero, of that there is little doubt

But what dark shadows may also be there- do they know what it's about?

They do not want to write of the aspects of war, that no one really wishes to see.

Perhaps if somebody dared to say, that which nobody says- the TRUTH?

It might alter the foolish perceptions of war- and avoid it for the future youth.

But this would be like shouting at the wind- like telling it not to blow.

For man has always killed his fellow man-why?

We'll not stop it-until we know.

Flanders Field

One hundred years ago on Flanders Field, men
were forced to sow

A different kind of crop, from which nothing good
would grow.

The fields would remain barren-although well
fertilised with blood

In winter ploughed by shell and shot-into deadly
clinging mud.

As men of many nations fought to reach a deadly
goal

The Padre shriving all- to save each soldier's soul.

But it could not be considered, as other than the
devil's day

Because here it was death and destruction- that
alone held sway.

This war of attrition, would appear to have no end

Until one side or the other had no more men to
send.

It only finished when another nation threw the dice

Deciding they had thousands of men they could
afford, to sacrifice.

With one side overwhelmed, at last a line was
drawn

In the hope of avoiding such a thing again- for
children yet to be born.

But in only twenty years, this was proven not to be

When 'still war weary' nations did a repeat of
history.

It appears that war teaches lessons, which mankind
will not accept

Because from his long experience at war, he
becomes ever more adept.

Frustration

The helmet hung on the upturned rifle, marks a soldier's lonely grave

just one more casualty, the medics could not save.

His dog tags are missing, do they even know he's gone?

It makes not the slightest difference; the war still carries on.

In war it makes no difference, it is just one individual life

but it's the only one that matters to family, lover, wife.

War is somehow impersonal but at the same time it is not,

War, so all destructive, can take everything you've got.

You've met your perfect partner, your future lies ahead

and then, nothing to do with you, a war is declared,

and without any warning your life is filled with dread

you have just found love, but you could end up dead.

It is suddenly so frustrating, because you have no say,

you have never been religious, but now you feel the need to pray.

But deep inside, you do not believe it could be true

these things happen to others, so it can't happen to you.

They say fight for your country, for your country's renown

but that's all wrong, you do your bit, not to let your comrades down.

Because when push comes to shove it's on each other you can depend

not on King and country, you rely on your friends.

In shared horror and danger, there grows a camaraderie

which, until you've been there, there is no way that you can see.

But at the same time, it is something we'd rather not experience

because mass murder of strangers does not make a lot of sense.

And it adds insult to fatal injury to die so far from home

and end up buried in a grave, marked 'identity unknown.'

14-18

It's the sound of marching men and it echoes from
the hill and glen,

it's the sound of men who were sent to war and
never marched home again.

It's the sound of gross incompetence and rank
stupidity,

it's the sound of leaders of men- who do not learn
from history.

It's the sound of a lost generation- the death of
dreams and plans and hope,

it's the sound of mothers and wives and lovers who
were left to weep and somehow cope.

It's the sound of exasperation, of soldiers who were
given no choice

it's the sound of frustration, of people who cared,
but had no voice.

It's the sound of destruction and mayhem, of
horror and death and dismay,

it's the sound of men, who for other's tomorrows-
sacrificed their today

The Sniper

Long Tom placed his sand-bag atop of the trench
wall

Each time he did he risked his life because he was
too tall

Bu Long Tom didn't worry, he did his job at night

But now the glare of a parachute flare, his face
reflected white.

Nearly half a mile away, out there in the night

A sniper turned to mark the spot where he had
seen the light

Slowly, oh so slowly, his gun moved in an arc

To realign where he had seen, that something,
shine out in the dark.

He settled back and waited, his gaze fixed way
ahead

The next time he saw something, that something
would be dead

But Tom had moved along to where a new gap must be filled

In innocence he did his job, instead of being killed.

But also in the darkness, but on the other side

Another sniper watched it all, from within his own hide

From the hunter was now hunted and he didn't even know

For when he moved, his rifle sight, mirrored the big glare flow.

He did not see or hear the shot that struck him in the head

One minute alive- alert- a second later, dead

So, the man who had killed so many since his job had been defined

Ironically was shot and killed by one of his own kind.

Trench-foot

Everybody knew that war was
Bullets, bombs and blood.
But none of us expected to
fight in liquid mud.

My boots were bulled and shining
when I exited the U.K.
but they were leaking badly
in just two months and a day.

My comrades told me that
I would end up with trench-foot
but I just laughed because
I never thought I would.

And then my feet were freezing
because they never did get dry

and if cold feet could kill you

then I would surely die.

My feet were white and swollen

my skin was peeling free

and I thanked god, the mud

didn't come up to the knee.

I ignored any victories

for death- I didn't give two hoots

for me, the highlight of the war

was getting better boots.

What They Really Were

On the eleventh day of the eleventh month
We assemble to recall
The men who for strangers, not yet born
Sacrificed their all.

Their names and ranks are on cenotaphs
In every city and town
But to give such meagre information
Let's our heroes down.

You would think these men did not exist
Before they went to war
But who and what they really were
Was in what they did before.

Major C.F Peters was a well-known architect
Private E.J Thomas, moulded clay to great effect

Private D.O Davies was a bread delivery man

Lance Corporal N.G Symonds sold wet fish from a van.

Second Lieutenant V.E Morse arranged a mortgage or a loan

Sergeant N.B Bates built homes of real stone

Private R.S Thomas worked on an assembly line

And every move he made- was done in measured time.

Another factory worker, Lance Corporal A.B Ford

Captain T.H Foster-Smythe was the son of an Irish Lord

Private G.C Williams drove an omnibus in Leeds

Private S.A Thomas supplied vegetable seeds.

Not many would mourn the death

Of Lance Corporal L.G Grubb

But many would miss good old Grubby

Who ran the Social Club.

David John had delivered the milk for years

And his loss more important by far

Than how and why the death occurred

Of an unknown Private D.J Carr.

To everyone who suffered loss – one main rule
applied

It wasn't Sergeant or Private so and so who had
died

It was David, Peter, Andrew, Adrian or John

Whose life had been forfeited and was forever
gone.

Lions Led by Donkeys

The Lions

The man on the poster has a big moustache

and an accusing, pointing finger

he said, 'Your Country Wants You'

it was better not to linger.

Besides, it was said, 'By Christmas

It would be all over and done.'

Better to enrol quickly

or else miss all the fun.

So, like lions roused from slumber

they queued up to sign on

unaware that with that signing

the lives they'd known were gone.

In droves they left their offices

and quit the factory benches.

They swapped their quiet, suburban lives

for a life of mud and trenches.

But they had naïve ideas

of what war really was

and saw it as romantic

to be fighting for a cause.

But as they neared the foremost lines

a change could be detected.

The things they saw and smelt and heard

were not what they expected.

The groundsheet covered bodies

laid out across the mud.

The wood and canvas stretchers

stained black with dried-on blood.

The pathetic rows of stumbling men,

each held by the man behind.

In a macabre game of follow my leader

for all but he was blind.

But it was in the eyes of the exhausted men

rotating to the rear.

When the new recruits saw something

that froze their souls with fear.

Then they were moving on again, up toward the
line

nobody had told them, but they could read the
sign.

The unremitting sound of war assaulted their ears

and every crash and every flash added to their fear.

The air was filled with smoke and smells

and sometimes death from exploding shells.

The noise and smoke and the screams of men

so, damaged they'd never be right again.

At last they reached the forward lines and were ordered into place

and some men were already dead without seeing the enemies face.

But this was modern warfare, and if they did survive

they be marked and altered for as long as they were alive.

But things were far, far worse, than the worst that they had ever feared

but they would still complete the job for which they'd volunteered.

The Donkey's

The same group of families
had managed every British war.
Thus, it was, they really were
the English Officer Co-op.

They were the landed gentry
and the aristocracy.
Although they still had power,
it was not what it used to be.

But they could still pull strings
within the British military
with decorated ancestors
in every family.
They'd served in South Africa
their grand-father's the Crimea.
And this new European war

would crown a fine career.

But the ways of war had altered
their knowledge no longer applied
the old guard was way out of date
no longer qualified.

But no one could dismiss them
their connections far too strong.
They would prosecute this war
no matter what went wrong.

It meant lions were led by donkeys
at least, so said the Hun.
Their opinion based on what they'd seen
since the war had begun.

A safe distance behind the line
they sighted G.H.Q.

And here the senior officers

decided what to do.

But this war had reached a stale mate

each army forced to stand,

on either side of ruined barbed wire,

filling no-mans land.

But the general knew mobile-fluid war

not this battle of attrition.

Thus, they had no answers

in spite of the king's commission.

They dreamt of a massive break-through

a cavalry led advance.

But that kind of war was out of date,

their dreaming had no chance.

So, they studied maps and charts and lists

laid out on the big map table, saying

'It would be good to take that wood,

if only we were able.'

'Then we could reach the river

and throw a bridge across.'

They calculated casualties

but not the real loss.

To them the troops were numbers

not men, with real lives.

With children, mothers, sisters, brothers,

tired, anxious wives.

On maps, the woods were near to where

the trenches came around.

But really it was half a mile

of open no-mans ground.

And the enemy had, had the time

to set up fields of fire.

For any who approached the wood

the outcome would be dire.

But fifteen hundred men were sent

and none of them returned.

They become one more statistic

with no new lessons learned.

Hundreds of children, fatherless

wives left to cope alone.

But however, many others fell,

HQ staff would all come home.

While mourning wives and families

who were left all on their own

found little comfort from the touch

of a cross of cold, white stone.

The Marksman

I became an army marksman through my own
ability

Where other men would stand and look, I would
stand and see.

For I was born a country boy and because of that I
could

See the land and how it lay, like townsmen never
would.

I was also gifted with exceptional good sight

It mattered not to me, whether the day was dull or
bright.

At seventeen I won prizes with someone else's
borrowed gun

What others took so seriously, I saw as just good
fun.

They would all practice daily, attempting to see

If they could learn to do better than I did
automatically

Then when the Great War started, I joined up with
the rest

As a soldier I was average, but on the range, I was
the best.

N.C.O.'S and officers would gather around to see

What their reports described as my 'superb ability'

Then I was informed that I would go to sniper
school

Which was far better than the front, so I thought it
was cool.

When there on my first morning I had to
demonstrate any skill

And they said, without any training, I could do a
long-range kill

But I told them, at the front I knew, it was death
and gore and mud

And I would take my chances there, I'd not kill in
cold blood.

They said I'd do what I was ordered, or face a nasty fate

I said they could order me to shoot, but you can't make me shoot straight

So, we were at a deadlock, I was too valuable to throw

Instead I stayed teaching others everything I knew

So, the army gained an instructor, who was second to none

A marksman who throughout the war, never killed a single one.

They Made Us What We Are

The 'Brits' are people whom it would appear, can't accept defeat

It's because they won't believe it, not even when they are beat

And if the unthinkable happens, as if on the rebound

Instead of giving in, they simply turn the whole thing around.

The Kaiser once called the B.E.F, a 'contemptible little army.'

And from that day forward, 'The old contemptibles' they would be.

In WW2, Tobrook's defenders, while surrounded, fought like cats,

And adopted it as their title, when the Germans, called them 'desert rats.'

In WW2 at Dunkirk, the B.E.F were surrounded

With no room to fight or resist attack

Hundreds of large and little vessels crossed the channel

To bring three hundred thousand veterans back.

Then came the typical British attitude

Dunkirk was a disaster, that was plain for all to see.

The men were welcomed back with the inevitable, a cup of tea

Then with aplomb they hailed the rescue as a victory.

But if you look at their ancestors, look at their bloodline

And it isn't really surprising, that they have turned out so fine.

All tough, fighting peoples, Celts, Saxons, Vikings, Romans, Normans, Angles

And the Brits have somehow managed, to evolve well from this big tangle.

Meanwhile this little island, which they are sure will never sink,

Built an empire which coloured, half the world map, British pink.

For centuries the Brits have punched above their weight,

And thus, not so long ago they were, the one, all powerful state.

How else could such a little nation have ever been labelled 'Great?'

The Contradictions

World War One started badly and went downhill
from there,

with men living in conditions, no-one should have
to bare.

Men were living and fighting, from holes dug in
the ground,

but a trench or shell hole was, the only shelter to be
found.

They exchanged a world of order, cleanliness and
calm,

to live with chaos, rats and mud, where other men
tried to do them harm.

And yet this was now the norm, old norms no
longer applied,

the standards by which they had lived till now,
were simply cast aside.

A year ago, to kill a man, was the greatest crime in
law,

but now it was the sole purpose, they had been brought out here for.

All of life's rules were altered, old standards swept aside,

morality non-existent and human values, callously denied.

In fact, things were just not altered, but actively reversed,

the man who would not fight or kill, the authorities now cursed.

The killer was now applauded, an aviator boasted of his kills,

his name was celebrated, his were highly valued skills.

Yet when all of this is finished, through the enemy's defeat,

he'd go back home and end up in court, for fighting in the street.

Where the very same authorities who had handed him a gun,

would look down their noses and say, 'This simply
is not done.'

These double standards see the law, crumble into
dust,

and incarcerate the hero who to the changes, cannot
yet adjust.

But this is the insanity, to which men regularly
contribute,

every rule and standard reversed, the minute it
may suit.

Thousands of years of civilisation, reversed to how
things used to be before,

because mankind still fails to find, an alternative to
war.

One Soldier's Story

He heard the call to arms and Kitchener's poster he
had seen

wishing to do his bit he volunteered, although not
yet eighteen.

The recruiting sergeant glanced at the smudged
birth certificate

no longer fit for active duty through poor eyesight--
he failed to read the date.

In weeks the basic training was all over and done

already fit, he had now learned to maintain and fire
a gun.

Taken by train and ship, all this to him was new

he'd not been on a train before--his comrades
laughed, believing it not true.

When they neared the front, to which they were all
new, he was no different from the rest

for all, their first encounter with war, their first
major test

But born to real poverty, he had grown up tough

and he thought things were still alright when the rest had had enough.

Warm clothes, good food were luxuries as far as he was concerned

he was half way there to start with, life's harder lessons already learned.

The others started to ask his opinion, a born leader as the officers say

and he'd stay put, and hold his ground, where others might run away.

Quite soon he was promoted but it didn't go to his head

and he went on surviving when others were hurt or dead.

He was a natural survivor, it was his was his natural in-built state

maybe nature's way of balancing--a way to compensate?

Unconsciously he adapted, to each new circumstance

where others saw a problem, he saw a great new chance.

He had unselfishly volunteered for what could have well been hell

but it had become an opportunity, through which he could do so well.

His unselfish action, for which he had falsified his age

had put him some where he fitted right in, a brand new clean life page.

As a professional soldier he felt alive

all that was required now, was simply to survive.

So, a war, which caused the sort of misery that only such a war could

for at least one poor, ex-unhappy misfit had really done some good.

Luck and skill saw him still standing, when the armistice was signed his friends and comrades left, but he was not so inclined

He became a lifelong regular soldier and thus, was still about

to help train the new young soldiers--when World War Two broke out.

Start as you intend to go on

Rows and rows and rows and rows
line upon line and so it goes.
In Belgium, France and Arlington
there lies the truth and proof of what's been done.
While in the First World War alone,
seventy-six thousand are laid in graves unknown.
Although great in theory, we have had to learn
there is a limit to how often the cheek can turn.
The problem is, that though you may wish for
peace,
the minority who do not, never seems to decrease.
The proof is there, to be seen in the passing years,
there is always a bully, to cause another child's
tears.
And even at this stage, supervision can fail
and a dictator is a bully, on a grander scale,
and while most look for peace, it's a bully's delight

to live by the thinking that 'might is right'

and as long as the mass is easily led

it is the members of the mass who end up dead.

With bullies you dare not turn a blind eye

because whenever we do, millions die.

The same rule must apply as in the school yard

when the bullying starts, you have to come down hard.

They Did Their Bit

It is obvious that war always causes change

this is inevitable, nothing very strange.

But World War One did far more than kill millions
of men

it ensured the world would never be the same
again.

The biggest change was to women's place in society

the old order was destroyed, and change was
wrought, that everyone could see.

The men were off and being killed, but the factories
still had to run

the war effort must continue, ammunition was
required for every single gun.

But the factories were only part, other businesses
like farmers had lost their labour too

and it was suddenly acknowledged, that the work
which needed doing, women were able to do.

What had been the employment positions when the men had ruled

were now being filled by women, jobs for which they had not been schooled.

The myth of male superiority was suddenly laid bare

but because of the war's necessity, society could not afford to care.

This change in the social order would add strength to the suffragettes

but in war this was not the time, the vote was coming but, not quite yet.

After the war returning men reclaimed the jobs that they had left

but the women were now emancipated, at men's work they had proved very adept.

Now women were expected to meekly return to how things had been

but they had changed for ever, this could be clearly seen

Before the war, women were domestic staff, chamber maids and such

but this had changed forever with politicians out of touch.

Women would soon be voting and have the first woman in parliament

the old order had changed which only a Luddite would resent.

The sons of landowners and gentry had been killed along with all the others

in many cases not just the eldest, but also their younger brothers.

The order of life and society was completely changed by nineteen eighteen

and it was changed forever, that was easily seen.

At last sexual equality had started, women could now show their opinion

now they had the vote, women's emancipation had really begun.

Suddenly their ambitions, which to men had always been fun

could make a difference, the war was over, and it was the women who had definitely WON.

The Unknown Soldier

I am the unknown soldier
Laid in my public tomb
I am Private, Corporal, Sergeant, Captain
No one knows quite whom.

I represent the fallen
In an unknown, unmarked grave
We are the proof that mankind's will to kill
Outweighs his skill to save.

But it's with the title 'unknown soldier' that I
disagree
For this label's me as a warrior, for all eternity
But I was conscripted – signed up for the duration
Removed from what I really was, to battle for the
nation.

I became an armed civilian

Along with all the rest

With a minimum of training

Sent out to do my best.

But one man in an army

Is like one leaf on a tree

You must know what you really are

Or lose identity.

I am a teacher, a preacher, an electrician

A milk delivery man

A miner, designer, jazz musician

Driver of a van.

It is true, my end was wrought

By bayonet shell or shot

And that I died in uniform

But a soldier I was not.

In rememberance our names are carved

On bronze and marble plaques

And although they add our army ranks

It does not change the facts.

It is not just the nation's warriors

Who fight to keep us free?

It's men with different skills who die

Civilians, just like me.

The End

Praise God it's gone eleven o'clock- the war is at an end,

I see a worthless field of mud, we've been dying to defend,

now at last I feel I can allow myself to doubt,

ten million men are murdered- what was that all about?

So how can any human quarrel ever justify

such carnage and destruction and let so many die,

and I ask myself, why is it that I've been spared?

When like all the others I was terrified and scared.

I was never any braver than I was forced to be

and death was really random, has fate been good to me?

I'm so relieved to still be here, complete in body and soul

While many thousand others are not even quite whole.

But I feel so very guilty that I have come through,

while better men than I have died- more than just a few

and now, at last we have peace, but oh, at what cost,

when you stop and think of the horrendous numbers lost.

And all of the pain and misery was not at the front alone

grief and sorrow, terrible loss, was also there at home

and all for what?

At the end of day, is this the war to end all war?

We can only pray.

The End Game 1915

We had all talked of volunteering and decided that
we should

But already the war had gone on longer than we
thought it would.

We all worked together and volunteered 'en masse'

We were all so idealistic, all as green as grass.

It was an adventure, some even thought it fun

Six months of something exciting and it would all
be done.

The training was soon over and we were set to go

But what we'd really agreed to do, we didn't begin
to know.

I remember the first shock I had, was the non-stop,
awful noise

And then we saw some casualties and some looked
only boys

For the first time we were frightened but by then it was too late

Had we eagerly lined up just to share such a fate?

But of course, we all pretended that we were not afraid

And that none of us regretted the decision we had made

But that was seven months ago and I am still alive

But being now a veteran, does not mean I will survive

Edward from the sales team was the first one to be killed

We were shocked, in training he had been the most skilled.

Then Thomas who was courting that blonde from the typist pool

Last week it was Harold, with whom I'd been in school.

Now the trench is full, we wait to hear the whistle blow

Twice we've failed to take that ridge, so we'll have another go

Were it not for the Germans, it would be an easy climb

Tomorrow I will write and say how we've done this time.

Now the whistles are blowing and I must lay down my pen

As soon as I return, I will take it up again.

They will never be the same

I am standing here and seeing an army moving past

but they are not marching or even moving very fast.

Are they all advancing or are they in retreat?

Have they won a victory? If so, is it one they can repeat?

They are not a very smart army, they are muddy and unkempt

ahead another assault awaits, another advance to attempt.

It seems to be never-ending, a daily struggle and grind

ahead of them are more hardships- with many comrades left behind.

Their boots no longer waterproof, their clothes are home for fleas

they are muddy, stained and threadbare at the elbows and the knees.

You can't look like 'parade ground' soldiers when you've been where they have been

they are muddy, dirty, scruffy, but their weapons are all clean.

Because these are real fighting men on whom freedom can depend

they will keep trudging on and on- right up to the end.

They had thought the tanks would end the war, but they kept on breaking down

but they know it must all end one day with relief, rather than renown.

They used to be clerks and carpenters, dockers and delivery men

perhaps when this is over, they'll go back to that again.

But at the same time, they are altered, they will never be the same

they have had to become tough and harder to survive the killing game.

How can they ever resume the mundane lives they left behind?

Many will never settle, so it's a new life they will have to find.

Because those at home won't understand the horrors that they have seen

and they themselves are haunted by what was, instead of what might have been.

The fighting will be over- the trauma will go on

the fear, the nightmares and the foolish guilt of their survival, when so many others are gone.

The Silent Sentry

A sentry who on duty does not tire

The ever willing, long lasting, barbed wire.

Barbed wire, such a simple tool of war

An instant barrier where nothing was before.

It appears so flimsy, haphazard, rusting stands

Yet can entrap and hold with iron hands

Its function, hold advancing enemy still

To give the defenders time to make a kill.

Spread and anchored low it will defeat

An enemy by catching at his feet

Or spread in spools, four-foot-wide Dannet coils

The opposing general's plan to thwart and foil.

Though, in time, years' rust will prevail

For ages in its duty, it will not fail

And even later on with peace it will somehow

Maintain its design and foul the farmer's plough.

This simple tool exceeds a hundred years of age

Is still in use, justifying its wage

In peace-time forms the boundary of a field

Apparently so frail it will not yield.

For years it stood alone but now inspires

A younger cousin- christened razor wire

Its function similar but it isn't quite

For this one causes wounds, it's full of spite.

But razor wire's main function is not in war

To enclose and hold prisoners is what it is for

For short containment, high walls are out of date

But for those who would crash through, lies a sad fate

The folly of such action, no one rebuts

For those who try, suffer a thousand cuts.

The Charge

The blowing of the whistle sends us on our way

For they will shoot as cowards, anyone who tries to stay.

So now we trudge through clinging mud, in a shell pocked, ruined field

It's supposed to be a rapid charge to force the foe to yield.

The noise, the smoke, the screams, the shells

Assault all of your senses

While physically you struggle to pass

Tangled, barbed wire fences.

The smoke is mixing with thick fog which helps hide our approach

As into no man's land we slowly encroach.

Comrades appear out of the fog and are just as quickly gone

We must be getting near there now, I keep
plodding on.

Two men simply vanish, in the explosion of a shell

And red-hot shrapnel rains on us like hail come
straight from hell.

The thick fog hides the carnage, that's happening
all around

But you can still hear it as you fight the muddy
ground.

A man just in front of me falls over stone dead

I see a random bullet has struck him in the head

I pass and look down at him, see shock frozen on
his face

And without realising it, I increase my pace.

Then my fears disappear, adrenalin's the cause

A man will need a lot of it if he is fighting wars

My senses are more heightened, the fog hides our
advance

If it stays thick for long enough, then we stand a good chance.

We step, like wraiths, out of the fog, the enemy ahead

I see the terror in their eyes as they are as good as dead

They drop their weapons, their shaking hands are raised

For now, the killing has been stopped, let heaven be praised.

I look into their faces, and it is plain to see

They are not beasts or monsters but young men just like me

With all the death and horror, a coldness fills my heart

Were it not for the uniforms, you'd not tell us apart.

It Cannot Go On

In my mind's eye set deep within my head

I see a million soldiers marching past

And they keep right on coming, they're the legions of the dead

Their lives were wasted, from first through to last.

The mix of uniforms they wear, make it very clear

Men of opposing armies all are marching here

It matters not what uniforms or badges they may wear

For death is not selective, it simply doesn't care

Death cannot be selective, it does not have a say

It just accepts the victims, that others send its way.

But now they are all comrades, as they march, side by side

Their enmity had vanished in the moment that they died.

And now they march together, there's no banner at
their head

No loyalty, no fear, nothing matters when you're
dead.

They also march together, having shared a common
fate

And if peace is made tomorrow, for them it is too
late.

For soldiers are expendable, although it's seldom
said

But if their lives are precious, why are so many
dead?

It's always the common soldiers, suffer the pain
and death in wars

And politician's failures always are the cause.

Some nations leader says that for him things aren't
right

Diplomacy has failed, the other nations must
capitulate or fight.

But politicians never fight, they rarely raise a hand

Seeing war as the 'has to be' result that circumstance demands.

This is how it's always been, down through every age

But at last things have altered, we are near the final stage.

Men must learn to live in peace, of that there is no doubt

Or else, with their modern weapons, they will wipe each other out.

Mankind must change, there must be peace, he must stop waging war

Or else the peace will come because, mankind will be no more.

Christmas 1914- The Medic

They lay where they had fallen, some still moving
in the mud

some were obviously alive, but all were losing
blood.

The bullets were still flying, whining overhead

the shells were still exploding but still--not all of
them were dead.

Then the medic crawled out--he had the red cross
on his arm

no other form of protection to keep him safe from
harm.

All of us were praying for him, because in the end

if you were hit and wounded the medic was your
best friend.

There were no German casualties--at least none that
you could see,

their wounded were all out of sight, already off to where they should be.

It was like a rule of war--always those attacking that were left in no-mans land

the defenders were still in their trenches--making their stand.

In war all soldiers are the same, their aim 'to stay alive'

and it appeared that 'Fritz' had seen his red cross-- and wished him to survive.

Because although the shells still kept coming--the crackle of small arms disappeared

as the nearest wounded man--the medic slowly neared.

We saw him give an injection and apply a tourniquet

then with no hesitation, he was once more on his way.

He treated another two, but then he checked and left two more and then he moved and started to help his number four.

Now a couple of others crawled out, to lend a hand

still no small arms fire--and we knew they could understand.

The wounded were no threat and one day it might be they

could be laying wounded and we would return, this favour that day.

In the midst of wars brutality, humanity raised its head

an act of human kindness--a few less soldiers' dead.

This little friendly incident was spontaneous-- totally unplanned,

who knows--by Christmas they may be swapping family photos--out in no-man's land.

You Cannot Take Anything for Granted

"Where are all of the soldiers"? the immaculate general said,

The muddy Sargent saluted and replied "--"The soldiers are all dead".

"Ridiculous" said the General "I' will get you more

without soldiers to kill each other, how can we have a war".

"It's a soldier's duty to kill the other side--until he himself is shot,

and in a good war like this is--we are going to need a lot".

The Sargent said "But what of you sir--you don't even have a gun"

"That is why I am a General--I have no need of one".

"Soldiers must have weapons with which to kill and fight,

but as a general I kill thousands each time I don't get something right.

You have to understand Sargent each class must do, that for which it is trained.

the upper classes rule and pass on orders-so that with a catastrophe--we really can't be blamed".

"Every General and field Marshal are of the upper classes,

we can't afford to have a war run by people who rise up from the masses.

We must maintain the status-quo we can't risk revolution,

the upper class is formed through our superior evolution.

It's our place to give orders--and yours to obey

to not accept your instructions--we will never see the day.

I order you to charge the enemy and you'll obey each word I've said" and the Sargent took up his rifle and shot the General dead?

They Led and they Bled

World war one was far more than just another war,

world war one changed everything--from how it was before.

It was the most horrendous, destructive war up until that time

and had triggered the beginning of--Great-Briton's decline.

Within a year of its end, we saw the first woman in parliament

and women would no longer be willing--to just be subservient.

Nearly all had lost someone, with somebody left to grieve--often a young wife.

But one group found-that through the war they lost--their entire way of life.

In 1914 they were the elite-A 'top university' educated--'upper class'

and when war broke out, they like thousands of others could not just let it pass.

So, in spite of the class differences they signed up with all the rest and put their lives upon the line to face--their most savage test.

But being who and what they were--upper class and well educated

it was they who had the background from which the future leaders were created.

While thousands of common soldiers were hit, fell down and bled

in every charge or attempted advance it was they who always led.

The average life of a junior officer was only six weeks-more or less

and these were the nation's future--educated with and by the best,

but they were the first over the top to face, the enemy's machine gun

often with the mud so thick that--they couldn't even run

and even more than the common soldiers they were annihilated

for bullets care nothing for ancestry--or to whom you were related.

Thus, many of the grandest families lost their first and second sons

and ancient ancestral lines were cut--before it was all done.

Bravely they blew their whistles--always leading from the front

doing duty for which they weren't properly trained--and didn't really want.

Those who survived, came home to a completely different land

and found they faced a future--nothing like that which they had planned.

Workers were in short supply--with an economy to rebuild

and there were better jobs than domestic staff, waiting to be filled.

The big houses of the gentry could not function without staff,

like Butlers, Gardeners, Cooks and House-maids-- all working on the owner's behalf.

Because of empty coffers--they'd married American heiress's--before the war began

but now the loss of sons and heirs there was little point, of their clever plan.

So, a privileged and traditional way of life, all came to a sudden end,

the changes wrought made it a way of life-- impossible to defend.

*Historian A.J.P.Taylor wrote;

"The slaughter of the subalterns in WW1 destroyed the flower of the English gentry. 12% of common soldiers were killed-----17% of junior officers--mortality rates were 65 to 80%, double that of the common soldiers. ETON alone lost 1,000 ex-students [Three years intake]."

Numbers.

At the start of World War One the British army was small,

it was really only a police force to serve, the colonies overseas.

While the continental armies were numbered in millions

Briton had not required such a force-for the duties they had done.

The UK army were all volunteers--no body was conscripted,

but with the start of the war, priorities had to be shifted.

Three thousand men a day volunteered from the day that they declared war

and all were going to be needed in just a few months more.

Later Kitchener's poster 'Your country needs you' saw millions volunteer together

and those who hesitated received the infamous white feather.

The army medical set very high standards, of fitness age and height,

they only wanted the healthiest being trained to fight.

But in just couple of years, the set of standards was decreased.

Because so many of the Kitchener's battalions had ended up deceased.

In nineteen sixteen conscription was introduced -- the lower age changed to eighteen

which gives an indication of the number of casualties there had been.

It appears it never occurred to the authorities that their policies could be wrong

they seemed to assume that the losses could just go on and on.

In another year or so would they reduce the age limit again?

Because without the Americans to tip the balance, all of the killing was in vain.

The battle lines hardly moved--much more than back and fore

did they think to go on sacrificing soldiers until there were no more?

Because other than that, it appears that there was no 'make peace' plan

except to keep their citizens fighting--if need be to the last man?

If this was the Government's thinking--there is only one thing to say

Thank god that the Americans had the Boston tea party--and thus formed the USA.

Will We Never Learn?

Whenever World War One is mentioned they recall
the horrendous numbers killed.

But there were twice as many wounded--their lives
left unfulfilled.

Limbs lost-blinded-disfigured on crutches or in a
wheel chair

minds destroyed by sights and things they could no
longer bare.

Against masses of machine guns ordered to
advance

their only protection a tin hat--thousands stood no
chance.

Through engineered patriotism they willingly
signed on

following the thousands who had already signed
and gone.

Wasted by politicians and generals wanting
victory--no matter what the cost

ending up resulting in so many young lives lost.

The horror of bodies buried by shell fire, then resurrected by the same.

With no real thought of compromise on any side--to everybody's shame,

and at the end of it all, what was it really for

to stroke the egos of kings and such--who should have gone many long years before.

The war to end all wars--was the one and only--promised gain

but just twenty-one years on and military bands played the same old refrain.

By the end of world war two, the ability to destroy advanced to such a degree

that if there is a world war three--the resulting aftermath may have no one left to see?

Make of It What You Wish

Most people enjoy a good story and because of this

from our childhood, a good tale is something no
one likes to miss.

But what of myths and legends, are they just tall
tales or facts,

did something special happen and the story tellers
react.

It isn't very often such tales can be verified

the facts being proven, the story not denied.

But in world war one such a thing occurred,

for proof of the story, doubters to the history books
are referred.

In nineteen sixteen the town of Albert in France

stood right in the path of the German advance.

The town's cathedral was topped by a large statue-
instead of a spirer

and in the nearby battle it was hit by German shell fire.

The statue of the Virgin Mary tipped and all but fell

just why it hung and did not fall, nobody could tell

it hung and was a danger--and could fall any day

and the story circulated--that there, it was going to stay.

The legend then circulated that it would stay suspended

protecting the town from conquest until the war was ended.

On the night of November, the tenth in nineteen eighteen--just as the legend said

the statue fell to the ground--and within hours there were no more soldier's dead.

The Extra Enemies.

In the spring of nineteen eighteen the Germans took the view

that they had to quickly win the war--the fresh American troops were due.

So, the stalemate was broken with by a sudden massive attack--that might well win the war,

and so, thousands of eighteen-year olds were sent to France--this had never happened before.

These young men went believing that they knew who the enemy was

not knowing that there was more than one--to know, would have given them pause.

Of course, the Germans were the main enemy-- pushing forward for all to see,

it was when in real action they realised--they had more than one enemy.

A second battle had to be fought with their sheer exhaustion, for once a battle had started, real sleep was at a premium.

The constant stress and fear, and Adrenalin when required

produced the sort of exhaustion which was way past falling down tired

and until they were rotated there was very little relief

while all of the time the nagging knowledge, that they could suddenly come to grief.

Another unexpected opponent was the ever-present thirst

they'd all been trained--but how to handle, a bone-dry mouth and throat had never been rehearsed

The water bottles they carried in battle-emptied really fast

whereas if not in action, one bottle would last and last.

While in winter the ground was frozen really deep and hard

and trenches had to be dug by the mile--never by the yard.

Then came the thaw bringing mud--through which you could not run

and you needed to be able to move really fast-- when facing a machine-gun.

So, all the soldiers became aware there was more than one foe to beat

they also had thirst, exhaustion and a harsh environment to defeat.

Such multiple terrible conditions took war to a new category

and they'd have to defeat them all--to securer, the longed-for victory.

The Extra Enemies.

In the spring of nineteen eighteen the Germans
took the view

that they had to quickly win the war--the fresh
American troops were due.

So, the stalemate was broken with by a sudden
massive attack--that might well win the war,

and so, thousands of eighteen-year olds were sent
to France--this had never happened before.

These young men went believing that they knew
who the enemy was

not knowing that there was more than one--to
know, would have given them pause.

Of course, the Germans were the main enemy--
pushing forward for all to see,

it was when in real action they realised--they had
more than one enemy.

A second battle had to be fought with their sheer
exhaustion,

for once a battle had started, real sleep was at a premium.

The constant stress and fear, and Adrenalin when required

produced the sort of exhaustion which was way past falling down tired

and until they were rotated there was very little relief

while all of the time the nagging knowledge, that they could suddenly come to grief.

Another unexpected opponent was the ever-present thirst

they'd all been trained--but how to handle, a bone-dry mouth and throat had never been rehearsed

The water bottles they carried in battle-emptied really fast

whereas if not in action, one bottle would last and last.

While in winter the ground was frozen really deep and hard

and trenches had to be dug by the mile--never by the yard.

Then came the thaw bringing mud--through which you could not run

and you needed to be able to move really fast-- when facing a machine-gun.

So, all the soldiers became aware there was more than one foe to beat

they also had thirst, exhaustion and a harsh environment to defeat.

Such multiple terrible conditions took war to a new category

and they'd have to defeat them all--to securer, the longed-for victory.

Uncovered

It was the falling rain that caused the mud

and the falling shells and shrapnel that brought forth the blood.

To shelter from the rain, you could not fail

but there was no shelter from the harsher hail,

it lashed like hail stones on the hats of tin

designed to protect the precious head within.

While only cotton and wool covered the rest

a failing cover when put to the test.

While knights of old were better protected than soldiers are today

armour that a sword stroke or axe blow could maybe stay

left the wearer with a fair chance to keep fighting and survive.

To-days soldier's only hope, is his enemy inaccurate marksmanship--may just leave him alive?

*During the period when British soldiers were in action in Iraq and Afghanistan, I was very moved by the regular sight on television, nearly every evening, of coffins of soldiers being brought home by Hercules transports and driven by a series of hearses through the town while the town's population lined the streets in silent respect. It was this experience that prompted him to write his protest poem--WHY. *

Why?

As I switch the television on I hear the word deceased

another soldier murdered out in the middle east.

The politicians tell us 'it's a job that must be done'

But I see no tears falling for some politician's son.

Eighteen- nineteen- twenty, what was this young man's age

who dared to close his Book of Life at such an early age?

These men are all volunteers, they are willing to defend their loved ones

and their country, though it could well mean their end.

But this is not what's happening, these young men did not fall

defending our beaches at Brighton or Porthcawl.

They died beside some foreign field, the question asked is why were they out there in the first place, let alone out there to die.

We cannot let our soldier's die in someone else's wars

nor should they be sacrificed for some yet, unproven cause.

Like Vietnam, where a superpower, attempted to impose

it's will upon the peasants and received a bloody nose.

Thirty full years later and all that the U.S feared

and spent its young men's lives on has not even appeared.

The politicians may tear their clothes, heap ashes on their heads

but no matter how they spin it, these young men are still dead.